Passive Income for Life or Retirement

What it is, Why you need it,
and ways you can get it.

James B. Fannin

Contents

Introduction

Definition of Passive Income

Passive income is a type of income earned with little to no effort on the part of the recipient. This income is generated through various methods, including investments, rental properties, and online businesses. The key characteristic of passive income is that it provides a steady stream of revenue without requiring the recipient's active participation in the income generation.

One of the most commonly cited definitions of passive income is provided by Robert Kiyosaki, the author of the book "Rich Dad Poor Dad." According to Kiyosaki, passive income is "money that comes in whether you work or not." This definition highlights the key characteristic of passive income: it provides a steady stream of revenue even when the recipient is not actively participating in generating the income.

There are several types of passive income, and each is generated through a different method. Some common forms of passive income include rental, dividend, and interest income. Rental income is generated through the ownership of rental properties, while dividend income is generated through the ownership of stocks and mutual funds. Interest income is generated through the ownership of bonds and other fixed-income investments.

Another common form of passive income is online businesses, such as blogs, YouTube channels, and podcasts. These businesses generate income through advertising, sponsorships, and affiliate marketing. Online businesses can provide a significant source of passive income, as they can reach a large audience and generate a steady stream of revenue with little to no effort on the owner's part.

It is important to note that passive income is not the same as residual income. Residual income is a type of income generated through a recurring business, such as network marketing or direct sales. Unlike passive income, residual income requires the active participation of the recipient in the income generation.

Passive income is an attractive concept for many people, as it provides a way to generate revenue by leveraging their time and effort without actively participating in generating the income. This type of income can provide a significant source of financial stability and independence, allowing people to achieve their financial goals and live the life they want.

In conclusion, passive income is any income earned with little to no effort on the part of the recipient. It is generated through various methods, including investments, rental properties, and online businesses. Passive income provides a steady revenue stream, allowing people to achieve their financial goals and live the life they want. By understanding the definition of passive income, people can explore the different ways to generate this type of income and take control of their financial future.

Why Passive Income is Important for Acquiring Wealth and Retirement

Passive income is an essential tool for acquiring wealth and achieving financial independence. Passive income provides a steady revenue stream, allowing individuals to build wealth over time and achieve their financial goals. This section will explore why passive income is essential for acquiring wealth and retirement.

1. **Financial Stability:** One of the real benefits of passive income is that it provides financial stability. Unlike active income, which is earned through a traditional job, passive income is not subject to the ups and downs of the economy, nor is it limited to the hours you can work. This benefit means that even during difficult economic times, individuals who have established passive income streams can continue to earn a steady stream of revenue, allowing them to maintain their financial stability and independence.

2. **Building Wealth Over Time:** Passive income provides a way to build wealth over time. Passive income is generated through investments, rental properties, and online businesses, which can provide a steady revenue stream for years or even decades. Individuals can build wealth over time and achieve their financial goals by investing the income from these income-generating assets and allowing it to compound, effectively multiplying its growth beyond the original income.

3. **Improving Cash Flow**: Passive income can improve cash flow, which is essential for financial independence. By having a steady stream of passive income, individuals can have more money available to pay their bills, save for retirement, and invest in other income-generating assets. Improved cash flow can also reduce financial stress and allow individuals to live more comfortably.

4. **Achieving Financial Independence:** Passive income is an essential component of financial independence. By having a steady stream of passive income, individuals can achieve financial independence because they are no longer dependent on a traditional job for a paycheck. This allows them to live the life they want without having to worry about their financial situation.

5. **Achieving Retirement Goals:** Passive income is also vital for achieving retirement goals. Many people rely on traditional sources of retirement income, such as pensions and Social Security, which may not provide enough income to maintain their standard of living in retirement. By building a portfolio of passive income streams, individuals can supplement their traditional sources of retirement income and achieve their retirement goals.

In conclusion, passive income is essential for acquiring wealth and achieving financial independence. Passive income is an essential component of a well-rounded financial plan by providing financial stability, allowing individuals to build wealth over time, improving cash flow, and enabling individuals to achieve financial independence and retirement goals. By understanding the importance of passive income, individuals can take control of their financial future and achieve their financial goals.

Importance of Diversification in Building Passive Income Streams

Diversification is critical to building a strong and sustainable portfolio of passive income streams. By spreading investments across multiple assets and sources of income, individuals can reduce their overall risk and increase their chances of success in generating passive income. This section will explore the importance of diversification in building passive income streams.

1. **Reducing Risk:** One of the main benefits of diversification is that it helps to reduce risk. By spreading investments across multiple assets and sources of income, individuals can minimize the impact of any one investment that may underperform. This benefit helps reduce the portfolio's overall risk and increase the likelihood of success in generating passive income.

2. **Increasing Returns:** Diversification can also help to increase returns. By investing in various assets and sources of income, individuals can benefit from the growth of multiple investments, leading to higher overall returns. By diversifying, individuals are more likely to achieve their financial goals and build wealth over time.

3. **Managing Volatility:** Diversification is also important in managing volatility. Different types of investments and sources of passive income can experience different levels of volatility, which can impact the overall stability of the portfolio. By diversifying investments, individuals can help to manage volatility and maintain a stable source of passive income.

4. **Protecting Against Inflation:** Diversification is also crucial in protecting against inflation. Inflation can erode the purchasing power of passive income over time. By investing in various unrelated assets and sources of income, Individuals can potentially reduce the impact of inflation on their passive income streams.

5. **Minimizing the Impact of Economic Downturns:** Diversification can also help minimize economic downturns' impact. By spreading investments across multiple assets and sources of income, individuals can potentially reduce the impact of any one investment that may be affected by a downturn in the economy. Diversifying into unrelated assets can help to maintain a stable source of passive income during difficult economic times.

In conclusion, diversification is vital to building a strong and sustainable portfolio of passive income streams. By reducing risk, increasing returns, managing volatility, protecting against inflation, and minimizing the impact of economic downturns, diversification can help individuals achieve their financial goals and build wealth over time. Individuals can effectively build their passive income streams and achieve financial independence by understanding the importance of diversification.

Renting Real Estate Properties

Residential and Commercial Properties Intro

Renting real estate properties can be an effective way to generate passive income. The rental market includes residential and commercial properties, each with its unique set of benefits and challenges. This section will explore the opportunities and considerations for investing in residential and commercial properties.

Residential Properties

Residential properties include single-family homes, apartments, and condominiums rented to individuals for residential purposes.

1. **Benefits of Residential Properties:** Residential properties can offer several benefits for investors looking to generate passive income. For example, residential properties are typically in high demand and offer relatively stable rental income. Additionally, residential properties are typically easier to manage than commercial properties and may require less maintenance and upkeep.

2. **Considerations for Residential Properties:** There are also several considerations that investors should keep in mind when investing in residential properties. For example, a residential property's value can be impacted by factors such as the local housing market, changes in the local economy, and competition from other rental properties in the area. Additionally, investors must manage the property, including finding and vetting tenants, collecting rent, and performing maintenance and repairs. Alternatively, you might hire a property manager, which will, at a minimum, reduce profits and could cost more than the potential profits.

Commercial Properties

Commercial properties include office buildings, retail spaces, and industrial buildings rented to businesses for commercial purposes.

1. **Benefits of Commercial Properties**: Commercial properties can offer several benefits for investors looking to generate passive income. For example, commercial properties typically offer higher rental income compared to residential properties and may also offer the potential for long-term leases. Additionally, commercial properties may offer a more predictable rental income, as businesses are less likely to vacate the property than individuals who may move.

2. **Considerations for Commercial Properties:** There are also several considerations that investors should keep in mind when investing in commercial properties. For example, the value of a commercial property can be impacted by factors such as the local business climate, changes in the local economy, and competition from other commercial properties in the area. Additionally, investors must be prepared to manage the property or hire a property manager who may not be cost-ef-

fective. Managing may include finding and vetting tenants, collecting rent, and performing maintenance and repairs.

In conclusion, renting real estate properties can be an effective way to generate passive income. Residential and commercial properties have their unique set of benefits and challenges, and investors should carefully consider these factors when choosing which type to invest in. By understanding the opportunities and considerations for residential and commercial properties, investors can take an informed approach to build their passive income streams through real estate investments.

The Advantages of Renting Properties

Renting properties can offer many advantages for investors looking to generate passive income. This section will explore some of the key benefits of renting properties.

1. **Steady Stream of Income:** One of the most significant advantages of renting properties is the potential for a steady stream of passive income. Unlike other investment vehicles, such as stocks or bonds, rental properties offer the potential for regular and consistent rental income. Rental income can provide investors with a reliable source of passive income, which can be particularly beneficial for those looking to supplement their income in retirement.

2. **Potential for Appreciation:** In addition to the steady stream of rental income, rental properties also have the potential for appreciation. As the property's value increases over time, investors can enjoy a growing return on their investment. Appreciation will affect rental income, which, together with the property's increased value, can provide a valuable source of passive income and a hedge against inflation.

3. **Tax Benefits:** Investing in rental properties can also offer several tax benefits. For example, investors may take advan-

tage of deductions for mortgage interest, property taxes, and maintenance expenses. Additionally, rental income is taxed at a lower rate than earned income, which can provide investors with significant tax savings.

4. **Control over Investment:** Another advantage of investing in rental properties is investors' control over their investments. Unlike other investment vehicles, such as mutual funds or index funds, investors can make decisions about the property, such as choosing the type of property, location, and tenants. This option can give investors greater control over their investment and the potential for higher returns.

5. **Tangible Asset:** Finally, rental properties represent a tangible asset that investors can touch, feel, and see. A tangible asset can provide a sense of security for investors, as they have a physical asset that they can rely on for passive income. Additionally, rental properties can offer the potential for legacy building, as the property can be passed down to future generations.

In conclusion, renting properties can offer many advantages for investors looking to generate passive income. From a steady stream of rental income to tax benefits and control over the investment, renting properties can provide investors with a valuable source of passive income. By understanding the advantages of renting properties, investors can make informed decisions about building their passive income streams through real estate investments.

Tips for Successfully Managing Rental Properties

Managing rental properties can be complex and time-consuming, but using the right strategies and tools can be a lucrative source of passive income. This section will discuss some tips for successfully managing rental properties.

1. **Screen Tenants Thoroughly:** One of the essential tasks in managing rental properties is selecting the right tenants. It is essential to screen tenants thoroughly to ensure that you have responsible, reliable tenants. This task includes conducting background checks, credit checks, and checking references. Additionally, it is crucial to set clear expectations and guidelines for tenants, such as rent payment due dates and maintenance responsibilities.

2. **Establish a Maintenance Plan:** It is vital to establish a regular maintenance plan to keep your rental properties in good condition. This plan should include regularly inspecting the properties, addressing necessary repairs, and performing routine maintenance tasks like landscaping and cleaning. By maintaining the properties, you can help ensure they remain attractive to tenants and retain their value over time.

3. **Implement Effective Marketing Strategies:** Another essential aspect of managing rental properties is effectively marketing your properties to attract tenants. This strategy can include utilizing online listings, local classifieds, and social media to reach potential tenants. Additionally, it is important to stage the properties, create high-quality photos and videos, and offer competitive rental rates to attract tenants.

4. **Use Technology to Streamline Management:** In today's digital age, there are several tools and technologies available to help streamline the management of rental properties. For example, property management software can help automate rent collection, maintenance tracking, and tenant screening tasks. Additionally, online platforms can help you communicate with tenants and receive payments electronically, saving time and reducing potential errors.

5. **Hire a Professional Property Manager:** If managing rental properties becomes too time-consuming or challenging,

consider hiring a professional property manager. A property manager can handle various tasks, such as rent collection, maintenance, and tenant relations, freeing up your time to focus on other aspects of your investment portfolio. Although it reduces your profit, it is how your rental property becomes even more "passive."

In conclusion, managing rental properties can be complex and time-consuming, but with the right strategies and tools, it can be a lucrative source of passive income. By thoroughly screening tenants, establishing a maintenance plan, implementing effective marketing strategies, using technology to streamline management, and hiring a professional property manager if necessary, you can help ensure the success of your rental property investments.

Investing in Stocks, Bonds, and Mutual Funds

Understanding Stocks, Bonds, and Mutual Funds

Investing in stocks, bonds, and mutual funds is a popular way to build passive income streams. This section will discuss the basics of these investment vehicles, including their advantages and disadvantages, so you can make informed decisions about which options may be suitable for you.

1. **Stocks:** Stocks are ownership shares in a company. When you purchase a stock, you effectively become a part-owner in that company and have a claim on a portion of its earnings and assets. Stocks offer the potential for high returns but come with higher risks.

2. **Bonds:** Bonds are debt securities issued by companies or governments. You are essentially lending money to the issuer when you purchase a bond. In exchange, you receive periodic interest payments and the return of your principal when the bond matures. Bonds generally offer lower returns than stocks but come with lower risks.

3. **ETF Funds:** ETF funds are investment vehicles that trade a pool of selected stocks, vs. mutual funds, which pool money from multiple investors to purchase a diverse portfolio of stocks, bonds, and other securities. ETFs are often considered better investments than mutual funds because they trade like stocks. On the other hand, mutual funds make only one trade a day, limiting investment strategies and flexibility. The differences in management may account for the difference in returns, perceived safety, and an investor's preference for a mutual fund over an ETF. However, ETFs typically have lower expenses and are generally more flexible investments. Like with a mutual fund, investing in an ETF fund can gain exposure to a wide range of assets and diversify your portfolio while reducing your overall risk.

Summary of Advantages and Disadvantages of Investing In the Market

1. **Advantages of Investing in Stocks:** One of the primary advantages of investing in stocks is the potential for high returns. Historically, stocks have outperformed other investment vehicles, such as bonds, over the long term. Additionally, owning stocks gives you the potential to benefit from the growth and success of the companies in which you are invested.

2. **Disadvantages of Investing in Stocks:** The high returns potential of stocks comes with higher risks. The value of stocks can be affected by various factors, including economic conditions, changes in the stock market, and the financial performance of individual companies. Additionally, investing in individual stocks can be time-consuming and requires a deep understanding of financial markets and the companies you select for investment.

3. **Advantages of Investing in Bonds:** Bonds offer the potential for steady, predictable returns, making them a popular choice for individuals looking to build a stable, passive income stream. Additionally, bonds can provide a source of income during economic uncertainty, as they often hold their value better than stocks during market downturns.

4. **Disadvantages of Investing in Bonds:** While bonds offer lower risk than stocks, they also come with lower returns. Additionally, the value of bonds can be affected by changes in interest rates, and in the event of a default by the issuer, bondholders may not recover their principal.

5. **Advantages of Investing in ETFs:** ETF funds offer the potential for diversification and professional management, which can help reduce risk and increase returns. Additionally, ETF funds can provide exposure to a wide range of assets and investment strategies, making it easier for individual investors to build a diversified portfolio.

6. **Disadvantages of Investing in ETFs:** One of the primary disadvantages of investing in mutual funds is the potential for high fees, which can eat into returns. Likewise, ETF funds have varying expense fees and may be subject to market risk. Further, similar to a mutual fund, the performance of the ETF fund may not always align with your individual investment goals. Although this writer believes ETFs are generally better for most investors, fees, and alignment with your goals may be subject to change. Both require monitoring to ensure they fit your overall plan.

Stocks, bonds, and ETF funds are all viable options for building passive income streams. By understanding the basics of these investment vehicles and considering their advantages and disadvantages, you can make informed decisions about which options may be right for you. It is also important to seek professional advice, as investing in stocks, bonds, and ETF funds carry a certain level of risk and requires a deep understanding of financial markets and investment strategies.

The Benefits of Investing in the Stock Market

Investing in the stock market is a popular way to build passive income streams and grow wealth over the long term. This section will discuss the benefits of investing in the stock market, including the potential for high returns, diversification, and professional management.

1. **Potential for High Returns:** One of the primary benefits of investing in the stock market is the potential for high returns. Historically, the stock market has delivered average returns of around 10% per year, outpacing other investment vehicles such as bonds and real estate. Additionally, the stock market offers the potential for long-term growth, allowing you to compound your returns over time and grow your wealth.

2. **Diversification:** Investing in the stock market allows you to diversify your portfolio and spread your risk across a wide range of assets. By investing in a variety of stocks, you can reduce your exposure to any one company or industry and minimize your risk. Additionally, investing in a mix of domestic and international stocks can provide even greater diversification, as the performance of different markets is often uncorrelated.

3. **Professional Management:** Investing in the stock market allows you to benefit from the expertise of professional money managers. By investing in mutual funds or exchange-traded funds (ETFs), you can gain exposure to a diverse portfolio of stocks and have your investments professionally managed, reducing the time and effort required to manage your investments yourself.

4.   **Liquidity:** The stock market is a highly liquid investment ve-
hicle, allowing you to quickly buy and sell stocks at any time.
This liquidity makes it an attractive option for individuals
needing access to their money in the short term, as it allows
you to quickly and easily convert your investments into cash.

5. **Potential for Income:** Investing in stocks can also provide a
source of income through dividends, which are company
payments to their shareholders. Additionally, stocks have the
potential for capital gains, as the value of the stocks you own
may increase over time. This combination of income and capital
appreciation can provide a powerful source of passive income.

However, it is essential to note that investing in the stock market
carries risk, and there is no guarantee of returns. Additionally, the
stock market can be subject to market volatility, and the value of your
investments may fluctuate in response to changes in economic conditions and other factors.

In conclusion, investing in the stock market offers several benefits,
including high returns, diversification, professional management,
liquidity, and income potential. However, it is crucial to understand
that investing in the stock market carries risk and that investing in
individual stocks requires a deep understanding of financial markets and investment strategies if you consider Investing in the stock
market. In that case, it is recommended that you seek professional
advice and develop a comprehensive investment strategy that aligns
with your individual financial goals and risk tolerance.

Tips for Investing in Stocks, Bonds, and Mutual Funds

Investing in stocks, bonds, and mutual funds can be a great way to
build passive income streams and grow your wealth over the long
term. However, it's important to approach these investments strate-
gically and well-informed to maximize your chances of success. This

section will provide tips for investing in stocks, bonds, and mutual funds to help you get started.

1. **Educate Yourself:** Before investing in stocks, bonds, or mutual funds, you must educate yourself on the fundamentals of these investment vehicles and the stock market in general. This education must include understanding how stocks, bonds, and mutual funds work and learning about different investment strategies and financial metrics. Reading books, attending seminars, and speaking with financial advisors can all be great ways to get started.

2. **Start Early:** The earlier you start investing, the more time you have to compound your returns and grow your wealth. Additionally, an early start allows you to take on more risk, as you have more time to recover from any short-term losses. So if you're going to start investing in the market, start now. Don't wait - start investing as soon as possible.

3. **Diversify Your Portfolio:** Diversifying your portfolio by investing in various stocks, bonds, and mutual funds is one of the most important steps to minimize your risk and maximize your returns. By spreading your investment across different asset classes and market sectors, you can reduce your exposure to any company or industry and help mitigate your risk.

4. **Consider Your Risk Tolerance:** When investing in stocks, bonds, and mutual funds, it's essential to consider your risk tolerance or the level of risk you're willing to take on. Taking risk into account will help you determine the right mix of investments for your portfolio and help you avoid taking on too much risk. Generally, individuals with a higher risk tolerance may choose to invest in stocks, while those with a lower risk tolerance may opt for bonds or mutual funds.

5. **Stay the Course:** Investing in the stock market can be volatile, and it can be tempting to make impulsive decisions based on short-term market movements. However, staying the course and maintaining a long-term perspective is essential. Historically, the stock market has delivered solid returns over the long term, and by staying invested and avoiding knee-jerk reactions, you can maximize your chances of success.

6. **Consider Professional Advice:** If you're new to investing or don't feel confident about your ability to navigate the stock market, consider seeking professional advice from a financial advisor. A financial advisor can help you develop a comprehensive investment strategy that aligns with your financial goals and risk tolerance and can provide guidance and support as you navigate the stock market.

In conclusion, investing in stocks, bonds, and mutual funds can be a great way to build passive income streams and grow your wealth over the long term. By educating yourself, starting early, diversifying your portfolio, considering your risk tolerance, staying the course, and seeking professional advice, you can maximize your chances of success and achieve your financial goals.

Creating and Monetizing Online Content

Types of Online Content
(Blogs, YouTube Channels, Podcasts, etc.)

There are numerous types of online content that individuals can create to generate passive income. Some of the most popular include blogs, YouTube channels, and podcasts. Each of these platforms offers unique benefits and opportunities for monetization, making them attractive options for individuals looking to build passive income streams.

Blogs are one of the earliest forms of online content and are a popular platform for sharing information, opinions, and experiences. They offer a variety of ways to monetize content, including advertising, sponsored posts, affiliate marketing, and the sale of digital products. Blogs can be created on a wide range of topics, making them a flexible platform for individuals with diverse interests and expertise.

YouTube channels are another popular platform for creating online content. They allow individuals to share videos on a wide range of topics, from cooking and travel to technology and fashion. Like blogs,

YouTube channels offer various monetization options, including advertising, sponsorships, and affiliate marketing. Additionally, YouTube is owned by Google, giving content creators access to a massive audience and the potential for significant revenue.

Podcasts have rapidly gained popularity due to their convenience and versatility. Podcasts are audio recordings that can be downloaded and listened to on the go, making them a popular choice for individuals who want to consume content while commuting, exercising, or completing other tasks. Monetization opportunities for podcasts include advertising, sponsorships, and the sale of digital products.

In addition to blogs, YouTube channels, and podcasts, there are numerous other types of online content that individuals can create to generate passive income. These include e-commerce websites, online courses, and mobile applications. No matter what type of online content you choose, the key to success is to create high-quality content that provides value to your audience and helps you stand out in a crowded marketplace.

In summary, there are numerous types of online content that individuals can create to generate passive income. Whether you create a blog, a YouTube channel, a podcast, or some other type of online content, the key to success is creating high-quality content that provides value to your audience and helps you stand out in a crowded marketplace. By leveraging the power of the internet and taking advantage of the numerous monetization opportunities available, you can build a solid passive income stream and take control of your financial future.

The Advantages of Monetizing Online Content

Creating and monetizing online content can be a great way to build passive income streams and establish a presence in the digital world. With the rise of the internet and social media, there has never been a better time to start creating and sharing your ideas, opinions, and expertise with the world. This section will explore the different types of online content you can create and monetize.

1. **Blogs:** Blogs are a popular form of online content that allows you to share your ideas, opinions, and expertise with a large and potentially global audience. To start a blog, you'll need to choose a blogging platform (such as WordPress), select a domain name, and begin publishing content. From there, you can monetize your blog by selling advertising space, offering products or services, or earning income from affiliate marketing. There are also ready-made blogging platforms, some free and some at a cost. The free sites generally give you less control, use your content for advertising, and offer limited control over the A.D. content. Paid blogging sites typically offer more, if not total, control.

2. **YouTube Channels:** YouTube is the world's largest video-sharing platform, and it's a great place to start if you're interested in creating and monetizing video content. To start a YouTube channel, you'll need to create a Google account, select a channel name, and begin uploading videos. From there, you can monetize your channel by earning money from ads, sponsorships, and merchandise sales.

3. **Podcasts:** Podcasts are audio-based content that can be listened to on the go, and they're a great way to reach a large audience interested in your topic or niche. To start a podcast, you'll need to choose a topic, create an intro and outro, record and edit your episodes, and publish them on a podcast hosting platform (such as iTunes, SoundCloud, or Stitcher). From there, you can monetize your podcast by selling advertising space, offering products or services, or earning income from affiliate marketing.

4. **Online Courses:** Online courses are a great way to share your expertise and experience with others while also earning pas-

sive income. To create an online course, you'll need to choose a topic, plan the content and structure, and film and edit your video lessons. From there, you can monetize your course by selling it on a platform like Udemy or Teachable or hosting it on your website and selling it directly to your audience.

5. **Social Media:** Social media platforms like Instagram, Facebook, and Twitter can also be used to create and monetize online content. For example, you can start a personal or business account and share your thoughts, opinions, and experiences with your followers. From there, you can monetize your social media presence by selling advertising space, offering products or services, or earning income from affiliate marketing.

It's important to remember that the key to successfully monetizing online content is building a solid and engaged audience interested in what you offer. To do this, you'll need to create high-quality content that provides value to your audience, engage with your followers and build relationships with them, and continually work to grow your audience and reach.

Tips for Successfully Monetizing Online Content

Monetizing online content can be a great way to earn passive income, but it's important to approach it correctly. Here are some tips for successfully monetizing your online content:

1. **Know your audience:** To monetize your online content, you must clearly understand your target audience. Who are they? What are their interests and needs? What are they looking for in your content? Knowing your audience will help you create content that resonates with them and is more likely to be successful.

2. **Provide value:** it's essential to provide value in your content to build a solid and engaged audience. Value means offering your audience something of value in exchange for their time and attention, whether that's information, entertainment, or some other form of value.

3. **Build a strong brand:** Building a solid brand is vital to monetizing your online content. Brand means creating a consistent image, voice, and message for your content that resonates with your audience and sets you apart from others.

4. **Diversify your revenue streams:** Don't rely on just one revenue stream when monetizing your online content. Instead, consider combining advertising, sponsored content, affiliate marketing, products, or services with building multiple income streams.

5. **Be patient and persistent:** Building a successful online content business takes time and effort. Be patient, focus on creating high-quality content, and don't give up if you don't see immediate results. The more you put into your content, the more you'll get out of it in the long run.

6. **Collaborate with others:** Collaborating with other content creators or businesses in your niche can help you reach a wider audience and monetize your content more effectively. For example, you could guest post on someone else's blog or offer to host a guest on your podcast.

7. **Utilize social media:** Social media is a powerful tool for promoting online content and building your brand. Use social media platforms like Twitter, Facebook, Instagram, and YouTube to share your content, engage with your audience, and build relationships.

8. **Measure and analyze your results:** Regularly measure and analyze your results to see what's working and what's not

working. Use analytics tools to track your audience, engage-
ment, and revenue, and adjust your strategy as needed.

By following these tips, you'll be well on your way to successfully
monetizing your online content and building a solid and profitable
business. Remember to create high-quality content that provides
value to your audience, and be persistent and patient.

Starting a Business or Investing in a Franchise

Types of Businesses and Franchises

Starting a business or investing in a franchise can be a great way to create passive income. However, choosing the right type of business or franchise for your skills, interests, and goals is important. Here are some of the most common types of businesses and franchises to consider:

1. **Service-based businesses:** Service-based businesses include everything from consulting and coaching to home repair and landscaping. If you have a specific skill or expertise, you may be able to turn it into a successful service-based business.

2. **Product-based businesses:** Product-based businesses involve selling physical or digital products. Products could include anything from handmade goods and clothing to digital products like e-books or software.

3. **Online businesses:** Online businesses are run primarily online, using platforms like Amazon or Etsy to sell products or services.

4. **Brick-and-mortar businesses:** Brick-and-mortar businesses are traditional physical storefronts that offer products or services to customers.

5. **Franchise businesses:** Franchise businesses are part of a more prominent brand and follow a specific model and set of guidelines. Franchises can be a good option if you want to own your own business but prefer to follow a proven model and have support from a larger organization.

When choosing a business or franchise, it's essential to consider your skills, interests, and goals. You should also consider the amount of capital you have to invest, as well as your level of risk tolerance.

Some other factors to consider when choosing a business or franchise include:

1. **Market demand:** Make sure there's a market for your product or service. Research your target market to understand their needs and preferences and ensure that there's a demand for what you're offering.

2. **Competition:** Consider the level of competition in your market. A high level of competition may make it more challenging to stand out and succeed, while a low level of competition may indicate a market is not in high demand.

3. **Growth potential:** Consider the potential for growth in your business or franchise. Is there room for expansion, or will you be limited in your ability to grow and scale your business?

4. **Support and resources:** If you're investing in a franchise, consider the level of support and resources you'll receive from

the franchisor. Resources could include training, marketing support, and ongoing operational support.

By considering these factors, you'll be better equipped to choose the right type of business or franchise for your needs and to create a successful and profitable passive income stream.

The Advantages of Investing in a Franchise

Owning a franchise can provide many benefits, including the potential for passive income. Here are some of the key advantages of owning a business or investing in a franchise:

1. **Control:** You control your financial future when you own or franchise. You're in charge of making decisions about your business, and you can earn as much as you're willing to work for.

2. **Flexibility:** Owning a franchise can provide you with greater flexibility. For example, you may be able to work from home, set your hours, or choose the types of products or services you offer.

3. **Tax benefits:** Owning a franchise can provide tax benefits. For example, you may be able to deduct business expenses and depreciation, which can help lower your tax bill.

4. **Potential for high returns:** If your franchise is successful, you have the potential to earn high returns on your investment. You may even earn passive income if you have employees or systems to run your business while not actively involved.

5. **Brand recognition:** When you own a franchise, you benefit from the recognition and reputation of the franchisor's brand. Brand recognition can help you attract customers and grow your business more quickly.

6. **Support and resources:** If you're investing in a franchise, you'll have access to support and resources from the franchisor. Resources can include training, marketing support, and ongoing operational support, which can help you run your business more effectively.

7. **Less risk:** Owning a franchise can be less risky than starting a business from scratch. You have less risk because you're following a proven model and have support from the franchisor, which can help you avoid common mistakes and achieve success more quickly.

8. **Increased income potential:** By owning a franchise, you have the potential to earn a higher income than you would as an employee. You're also in control of your financial future, which can provide greater financial security and peace of mind.

While investing in a franchise can provide many benefits, it's important to understand that it also involves risk. You'll need to invest time and money, and you may face challenges along the way. However, with the right approach and mindset, you can create a successful and profitable franchise and build a passive income stream that provides financial security and independence.

The Tips For Starting a Business

Starting a successful business requires careful planning and preparation. Here are some tips to help you achieve success:

1. **Conduct thorough research:** Before starting a business, you must research your options and understand the market. Consider your goals, skills, and interests, and look for businesses or franchises that align with your strengths and values. Research the competition and market demand, and assess each opportunity's financial projections and risks.

2. **Develop a business plan:** A well-structured business plan can help you stay organized and focused as you build your business. Your business plan should include your goals, target market, marketing strategy, budget, and operational plan.

3. **Seek advice from experts:** It's essential to seek advice from experts in the field when starting a business. Consider working with a business coach, accountant, or attorney to help you navigate the process and make informed decisions.

4. **Seek funding:** Starting a business typically requires significant time and money. Consider your funding options, such as loans, investments, or grants, and choose the option that makes the most sense for your needs.

5. **Be prepared for hard work:** Starting a business can be challenging and may require long hours and hard work. Be prepared for the effort and dedication it takes to succeed, and be willing to make sacrifices in the short term to build a strong foundation for the future.

6. **Focus on customer satisfaction:** Your customers are the key to your success, so it's essential to focus on their needs and satisfaction. Develop a customer-focused culture, and strive to provide the best possible customer service.

7. **Stay organized:** Keeping good records and staying organized can help you run your business more efficiently and effectively. Use technology, such as accounting software and project management tools, to help you stay on top of your finances and tasks.

8. Stay up-to-date with the latest trends, technologies, and best practices in your field. Attend trade shows, conferences, and workshops, and read industry publications to stay informed and gain new insights.

9. **Stay flexible:** Be prepared to adapt and change as your business evolves. Be open to feedback and new ideas, and be willing to make changes as needed.

10. **Seek support:** Starting a business can be a lonely journey, so it's essential to seek support from friends, family, and colleagues. Consider joining a business network or mentor program to connect with other entrepreneurs and get advice and guidance.

Starting a successful business requires careful planning, hard work, and dedication. With the right approach and mindset, however, you can build a successful and profitable business and create a passive income stream that provides financial security and independence.

Conclusion

Recap of the Different Ways to Create Passive Income

The creation of passive income is crucial to building wealth and se-curing a comfortable retirement. In this eBook, we have explored five ways to create passive income, each of which has its unique set of benefits and challenges.

First, we looked at renting real estate properties, both residential and commercial, and discussed the advantages of owning rental proper-ties, as well as tips for successfully managing them.

Next, we delved into the world of stocks, bonds, and ETF funds and explored the benefits of investing in the stock market and tips for investing successfully.

We then discussed the creation and monetization of online content, including blogs, YouTube channels, and podcasts, and provided tips for successfully monetizing online content.

Then we explored investing in a franchise, the benefits of owning a franchise, and tips for investing in a franchise.

Finally, we looked at starting a business and the steps needed to start a business successfully.

In conclusion, creating passive income is crucial to building wealth and securing a comfortable retirement. You can choose the method that best suits your needs and goals by exploring the different ways to create passive income.

Whether renting real estate properties, investing in stocks, bonds, and mutual funds, creating and monetizing online content, starting a business, or investing in a franchise, the opportunities for creating passive income are vast and varied. With careful planning and due diligence, you can build a solid passive income stream that will provide financial stability and peace of mind for years to come.

The Importance of Taking Action and Starting Today

Creating passive income is a long-term investment that requires time, effort, and patience. While it may be tempting to delay taking action, it is crucial to start today to maximize the potential for financial growth and security in the future.

By taking the first step and beginning to build your passive income streams today, you are taking control of your financial future and setting yourself on the path to financial independence. It is never too early or too late to start, so don't wait for the perfect moment to begin your journey toward building wealth and securing your financial future. Start taking action today, and watch your passive income streams grow over time.

Final Thoughts and Recommendations.

In conclusion, creating passive income streams is crucial to building wealth and securing a comfortable retirement. With the wide range of options available, from renting real estate properties to investing in stocks, bonds, and mutual funds, creating and monetizing online content to starting a business, or investing in a franchise, the opportunities for creating passive income are vast and varied.

We hope this eBook has provided valuable insights and inspiration for building your own passive income streams. We wish you the best of luck on your journey toward financial independence.

Author Bio

The author is a multi-talented individual with a wealth of experience and knowledge. He has written several eBooks, Word Search Puzzle Books, a 12 Week Bible Study, showcasing his extensive writing experience gained by training and corporate experience.

With a background in senior management positions and small business ownership, including rental real estate and online sales, he has proven his entrepreneurial skills.

The author previously held a Life and Health Insurance, Annuities, and Medicare License in Texas, adding to his diverse range of expertise. The author has also worked in I.T, where he was a Senior Support Specialist at the Administrative Office of the U.S. Courts, and in sales at Colgate-Palmolive, where he was a former Sales Manager. He also held the position of National Sales and Support Manager for Interactive Accounting Products at Automatic Data Processing and was a former Assistant Supervisor Regional Check Processing Dept. at the Federal Reserve Bank of Dallas. He has a B.A. degree in Theology and Psychology and has studied New Testament Greek at Dallas Baptist University, further enriching his knowledge.

www.ingramcontent.com/pod-product-compliance
Lightning Source LLC
Chambersburg PA
CBHW071121220526
45467CB00004B/1995